To Jo

and a New year full of intuition + Magic

UNLEASH
YOUR
INNER PSYCHIC

With love + blessings

Sashi Radley

Sashi Radley

Disclaimer: The information in this book is provided for entertainment and informational purposes only and not a substitute for professional medical advice. Use of the information within this book is at the readers discretion and risk. If you are suffering from psychological or mental health issues always seek advice from the appropriate medical professional before participating in any of the exercises. Neither the author, publisher or associates can be held responsible for any loss, claim or damage arising due to the suggestions made.

No parts of this book may be reproduced by any process, transmitted or otherwise copied for public or private use other than reasonable short quotations within articles or reviews, without the written consent of the author.

DEDICATION

for

Rex Reynolds

Dad

From whom I inherited my quirkiness,
my Celtic, Druidic, Bardic ancestry,
and my passion for all things mystical.

You believed in me.
Allowed me to embrace my individuality.
And encouraged me to be
the best I could be.

CONTENTS

Unleash Your Inner Psychic

ACKNOWLEDGEMENTS

I have been blessed to have the unwavering love and support of my wonderful husband Rick. Thank you for encouraging me and having patience with my constant need for feedback and critique. Without you, I would never have achieved this little book. You are my universe, and my rock!

My heart-felt thanks go out to the following:

Brighton based Illustrator/Animator, Mark Billington, for his wonderful uplifting cover design. Those, who read the original draft and gave their truthful constructive feedback.

My love and gratitude to my amazing sons, Simon and Mark, for their faith and belief in me. Paul and Patricia in NYC. My dear friend, fellow writer, Tania Kremer-Yeatman, for her time, honesty and our endless coffee fuelled, spooky conversations.

To my great friends, Mala, Brenda, Sue, and inspirational author and healer Anne Jones. You gave me the confidence to make this happen. To author, J E Rowney for her valuable formatting help.

Alyce – A whisper away.

To author and tutor, Della Galton and all my friends at her creative writing class. To Aimee for proof-reading and critique. Amanda Roussos for her encouragement and angelic input.

To Fred, my step-son for making sure I always had the tools for the job! To Josie, Nick, Zoe, Jo, Lizzy, Lily, Claire, Val and my entire family for their interest and encouragement.

To Earth Angel - Debs Atkinson who never doubted me and made me believe in myself and creative genius, Tom at Wizard Websites.

To Emma Avhede and all my clients and students, who put their trust in me on their journeys of discovery, shared their healing experiences, and nagged me to write this book.

Ellie for warming my heart and my feet while I wrote.

And finally - Gwen, my mum, always watching over me from above. Thank you all!

Introduction

We are born with instinctive understanding, amazing intuition, attuned senses and pure connectedness to the world around us. Then, we are taught to switch it off.

This book is about re-awakening our naturalness. Learning again to be at one with our environment and the energies which move around us. Re-awakening our senses to help us move through life making the right choices for us by using our intuition, and if you are keen - developing psychic abilities to guide and inform.

By re-igniting your natural state of knowing, you will begin to realise that the world epidemic known as `stress` is mostly caused by working against our natural flow.

This little book of exercises gives you step by step techniques to re-connect and re-boot your intuition, and if you wish - take the further step to tapping into your psychic abilities. It`s not magic! It`s a reminder of what you already know.

Whether you wish to utilise these forgotten skills to enhance your spiritual development, to become a psychic reader or medium or whether you wish to be more perceptive in a business setting, the exercises in this book are designed for you. They are intended to be fun, enlightening and simple.

After reading the introduction you can quickly launch into the psychic development exercises. With practice, they will lead you to re-connect to what is naturally yours in a safe and enjoyable way.

And by the way...... I knew you would pick this book up!

Chapter 1
Modern Day Knowing

This book is for you! You have been drawn to it. You picked it from the selection available. If your eye or hand, went straight to it and you are reading this – then maybe some unseen force guided you.

Your intuition is your constant guide. Some call it the higher-self, others call it psychic ability, for the sake of this book we will call it your natural ability - intuition. The awakening of your psychic skills comes, through first acknowledging the intuition and trusting and befriending it – then you will find your psychic awareness beginning to blossom.

If you look at the dictionary definition for the word `intuition` it will read something like this:
Instinctive understanding or knowing, without conscious analysis or reasoning.

The dictionary definition for the word `psychic` is slightly different: *Faculties or phenomena inexplicable by natural laws, such as the ability to predict the future or know what other people are thinking.*

For the sake of re-awakening your intuition and psychic abilities, shall we agree to keep an open mind and ask this question? What if it was your intuition that guided you to pick up this particular book from the vast sea of choice?

Most of us at some time will have experience of knowing who is at the end of the phone before answering - or thinking of a friend we haven't seen in years and then bumping into them in the most unlikely place. Is it synchronicity? Is it premonition? Is it sixth sense? Or, is it simply knowing?

I believe the exercises in this book work. They are designed to help us quieten our minds enough to perceive the world around us in a different, more natural way. The way our ancestors would have experienced their world.

The advent of the electronics era has created a generation of humans who have lost touch with their ability to utilise all of their senses. The constant whirr and buzz of electro-magnetic radiation, geopathic stress, mobile phone use and high caffeine intake has dumbed down our natural interaction with the world around us so much that we can no longer function instinctively.

As young children we are still very much in touch with our senses. We often perceive other dimensions which our adult counterparts have disconnected from many moons ago. At around the age of six or seven years we gradually begin to lose our natural awareness. We become conditioned to believe that the other worlds we once all had the ability to tap into are not real, simply figments of a childish imagination.

With games consoles, computer tablets and mobile phones being introduced so early in our development cycle we quickly block out all connection with the natural knowing we were born with.

Many multi-tasking parents admit that they sometimes resort to plonking their toddlers or pre-school kids in front of a computer tablet to keep them amused.

Today sixth sense becomes something to aspire towards. The irony of this – is we came in to this life with this wonderful natural skill. Were tricked into believing it unnatural, creepy, weird or outmoded and encouraged to discard it along with the tooth fairy in favour of technology and modern living.

We are born naked and quickly taught that our natural state of nakedness is wrong. We must wear clothes. We are born with intuition, natural psychic abilities, honed senses and pure connectedness to the world around us.
Then we are taught to switch it off!

Maybe we should re-educate ourselves before we become so robotic and shut down that we can no longer feel or experience the joy of real sensation.

I am not suggesting we all run around naked chanting, "I see a tall dark stranger – you will be rich beyond your wildest dreams" or "I can feel a grandfather figure coming through for you!" But it is such a natural state to be using all our senses and to be comfortable with it. If more of us tuned ourselves in, then maybe we could become more harmonious and empathic in our relationships through having a better awareness of what others were feeling.

My own psychic ability is something I learned to hide for many years. As with many other psychics, intuitives, mediums etc., my experience started with a childhood trauma. Between the age of 3 and 4 years old, I developed the life-threatening condition encephalitis, after a seemingly mild dose of chicken-pox. Encephalitis is inflammation of the brain. I collapsed, lost the use of my limbs, my speech disappeared, I was hospitalised and was effectively unconscious for 3 weeks. But I still have a strong recollection of everything which was happening in the hospital around me. I now realise that I had a near death experience – and whilst in my unconscious state I drew close to the spirit world.

Against the odds, I slowly recovered from my illness. I learned to walk and talk again but it was a very worrying time for my parents. I emerged with an awareness way above that of pre-illness.

It was scary for me too, because my parent`s fear was that I had received brain damage from my illness so when I shared my experiences, I was told that I was imagining things; that I was dreaming, that there was nothing or no-one there. It left me more scared because the people I looked up to and relied on to keep me safe didn`t seem to be having the same experiences. I learned to keep it to myself. I tried to switch it off.

When I reached my late teens, I began to have vivid dreams containing strong premonitions – which nearly always came true. At that point I knew this wasn`t going away. It was to be something that was with me for life.

I had to learn how to manage it and turn it into a gift. Denying it, was not comfortable so embracing it became the answer.

In more recent years, I have discovered so many people who have had their own psychic abilities unleashed after a life-changing trauma or near-death experience. Hence the desire to teach others to hone their skills and use them in a positive way was born. In my opinion, it is healthier to embrace them, than push them down.

Whether you believe in psychic abilities or not, most people are curious about the supernatural world.

You will most likely fall into one of the categories below:

- ❖ Believe for no reason.
- ❖ Believe because you have had an experience or encounter.
- ❖ Think it all nonsense - for no reason.
- ❖ Think it all nonsense - because you have had no personal experience.
- ❖ Think it all nonsense – because it is not scientifically proven.
- ❖ Open minded - but need it proved.

❖ Do not believe - because it is against your belief system.

❖ Believe - because you are already using your psychic abilities.

Whichever category you fit into, it doesn't really matter. Electricity cannot be seen with the naked eye without intervention. But we know it exists. The difference between that and the invisible energetic world around us is that in the past there has been no real benefit to scientist or religious organisation in proving its existence. And because the conditions to tap into your natural pool of knowingness need to be calm, relaxing and uninterrupted there have been few times when a psychic or intuitive has been able to prove their abilities under the stress of scientific scrutiny. It is sad that there is so much fear attached to having this natural knowingness.

Over hundreds of years, stories of being burned as witches has conditioned many of us into a fear state. It seems it is now built in at cellular level. But the truth is these latent abilities are a natural part of being human.
Let's switch them back on!

If you were told that your hearing or vision would be turned off because only witches could hear or see, would you think that acceptable?
Nope – me neither.

The world is changing – here in the 21st century we seem to be keen to move back to a state of naturalness. Meditation, yoga, energy healing, spiritual and psychic development seem to be becoming the norm. Yippee – now you can call me Norm!

As human beings we are all unique. Born with differing strengths and weaknesses. We are inclined towards a diversity of occupations, hobbies, careers. Our appearances are different, our likes and dislikes vary to a huge degree. Some are mostly creative, others lean towards logical, practical pursuits. Even if we all wished to be movie stars, sculptors, artists, we may not have the abilities to make it work. We gravitate towards what makes us tick. In the same way our intuitive/psychic perception manifests in a variety of ways.

Once you start to do the following exercises you will soon get to know which sense is predominant for you.

Although initially some of the exercises may not seem to have anything to do with developing your intuition. Trust me! They all improve your sensitivity, which then translates into heightened intuition or psychic abilities. Some may resonate more than others – but they all play their part in honing your intuition in order to **Unleash Your Inner Psychic.**

Chapter 2
Sensory Perception

On route to making itself known; our intuitive perception creates a physical response in the human body. Our intuition sends messages to the body by utilising the five senses, or six senses if you include `knowing`. The physical response is often very subtle, so it takes practice to recognise and acknowledge. The trick is to learn how to pick up on those subtleties.

We each have varying levels of perception. One of the first lessons is to establish what your strongest sense is.

How do you receive your psychic impressions? Through sight, sound, touch, taste or smell? Once your intuition is strengthened and your psychic abilities start to emerge you may find yourself being guided by more than one method of instinctive understanding. It`s always good to have back up confirmation. And with practice your intuition will become stronger.

Subconsciously, you have probably chosen a profession, career, hobby or path which already highlights your predominant sense. Once you have read through the following, take a few moments to contemplate whether your current occupation reflects which of the **Clair** categories you slip into, or cross over. So here they are:

Clairvoyance – clear sight or seeing

If you are predominantly visual in your everyday life, for example: In a learning situation, you take information in better when you can see it written down or as drawn images in front of you? If so, it is likely that when you tap into your intuition clairvoyance will be your strongest sense.

Those with clairvoyant ability are often vivid dreamers seeing their dreams clearly in picture form.

When this `perception muscle` is honed you may eventually receive accurate visions, past, present and future in your mind`s eye. With practice you can learn to interpret their meanings.

Clairaudience – clear hearing

If you absorb information and retain it better by closing your eyes and listening whilst in a learning situation, the chances are when developed, your predominant method of perception will be clairaudience. This is when you experience audible messages in the form of words, music or sound within your own mind.

Often you will receive words or sentences as if they were your own thoughts.

Clairsentience – clear feeling

Do you get a gut feeling, good or bad before something happens? Do you have such empathy with the plight of others that you sometimes feel overwhelmed?

If you are the one who mirrors aches and pains in the presence of someone who has those problems, or you pick up on the emotions of others immediately on meeting them, feeling it in your own body; then clairsentience is most likely to be your strongest sense.

Clairessence - Clairolfaction – clear smelling

If you have a powerful sense of smell and can detect odours that others often cannot, then this could potentially be your primary Clair. There are many terms for this particular Clair, including clairalience or clairolfaction.

Clairessence is sometimes interpreted as `psychic smelling`. If you have ever smelled cigar smoke, perfume or another aroma which had no obvious physical source then this could be an example of clairessence. It is possible you were detecting the presence of something or someone outside of your ordinary perception. Some refer to it as smelling the energy of spirit. Often medical intuitives (practitioners who psychically sense illness within the body of others) report being endowed with this Clair, which seems to be strongly connected with clairgustance, the taste Clair. This is possibly because, the senses of taste and smell are also linked under non-psychic circumstances. As a child, you may have been told to hold your nose whilst taking yucky medicine, you may remember that if you couldn`t smell it, the taste was lessened.

Clairgustance – clear tasting

If you have good taste buds and a heightened sense of taste in everyday life, then clairgustance could be added to your intuitive tool box. It is one of the rarest forms of sensing.

It can take its form as a taste when nothing associated is physically present. There have been many documented cases of medical intuitives detecting illness or deficiencies in a patient by an associated taste in their own mouths (often backed up by an odour). This may seem bizarre - but during pregnancy we accept that strange cravings are the body`s way of communicating its needs for mother and foetus. Clairgustance is the body`s way of intuitively letting you know on the behalf of another.

Claircognizance – clear knowing

This is the most difficult Clair to explain – it involves being in possession of psychic or intuitive knowledge without any prompt.

It is simply knowing! A truth which we know immediately and cannot explain its source, which then proves to be accurate.

Chapter 3
Relaxing your way to Sensitivity

The first tool for accessing your intuition is learning to place yourself into a relaxed state.

If you are someone who already meditates then you have a head start. If not, meditation is a way of quietening your thoughts. This enables you to access your subconscious mind or higher-self (the part of you which knows all the answers). By doing this it enables you to kick-start your power of knowing.

For this exercise you are going to relax your mind and engage your senses through a simple guided visualisation.

It is always important to ground yourself fully after any psychic work. That means – make sure you`re fully present and back to normal awareness when you finish.

Stamping your feet, clapping your hands or having a nice cup of tea and a chocolate bourbon biscuit all work well.

Please don`t try any of these exercises whilst driving or operating machinery or when you need to be fully aware or if you have any mental health issues.

Which Clair are you?

Take yourself to a quiet place where you won`t be disturbed. Have a pen and paper ready to make notes for when you have finished your exercise. You may wish to record the following exercise to a voice recorder before starting to help you engage completely with the process, but this is optional.

- ❖ Switch off your phone. Prop yourself up in a comfy sitting position with your back nice and straight.
- ❖ If sitting is a problem for you it is ok to lay down.
- ❖ If you struggle with switching off, then playing some relaxation music quietly in the background should help. Nature sounds, spa type music, music for healing, anything which has a soft rhythm to lull you into relaxation will do. Try not to go for anything with a melody as your conscious mind will start to engage.
- ❖ Close your eyes. Regulate your breathing. I call this **Breath Balance.**
- ❖ Start by emptying your lungs.

- ❖ Breathe out fully allowing the exhaled air to make a rushing sound through your mouth.
- ❖ Breathe in deeply through your nose. Hold your breath to a count of 7.
- ❖ Breathe out through your mouth to the count of 8.
- ❖ *Repeat*
- ❖ Breathe in through your nose. Hold your breath to a count of 7.
- ❖ Breathe out through your mouth to the count of 8.
- ❖ Allow yourself to relax into a rhythm.
- ❖ Once you have repeated your relaxation breathing cycle a few times - you will find yourself drifting. Continue to breathe in and out deeply at a comfortable pace.
- ❖ Throughout this little book – we will refer to the above as your **Breath Balance**.
- ❖ Now, imagine you are sitting in a coffee shop in the heart of London. You are at a window seat.
- ❖ Take your awareness to the sound of your own breathing. Do you notice any aroma`s associated with your location?

❖ Breathe in and out deeply, notice any subtle smells that creep into your nostrils as you look around the coffee shop.

❖ Breathe in and out deeply keeping that rhythm.

❖ Maybe you notice the door opening and closing as new customers come in. Is there any aroma drifting through the open door? Allow yourself to explore this experience completely.

❖ Are there any sensations within your body? If so where in the body do you feel the sensation?

❖ Do you feel happy, sad, elated, uncomfortable?

❖ Allow yourself to scan the environment. What do you see, if anything? Are the images clear or fuzzy? Are the images large or small? Do you see in vivid colour? Or are the images in black and white?

❖ Continue to regulate your breathing to a relaxed rhythm.

❖ Maybe you notice a red London bus outside the window. It`s engine is idling while passengers get on and off. Notice any sounds, smells, feelings, sensations associated with this busy scene.

❖ Take as much time as you need for this, don't rush. When it feels like you have explored the scene completely, give yourself a few minutes more, then start to take your attention back into your body.

❖ Feel the seat beneath you and the ground beneath your feet or the surface beneath your body. Wiggle your fingers and toes to bring your attention back into the present. Open your eyes.

❖ Before you become too alert, jot down onto your paper anything related to your experience.

❖ Based on your notes go back to the list of Clairs above and see if you can work out which is your dominant sense of perception.

❖ If you could really smell, see, taste, feel etc., this will give you a better idea of which of these are your strengths.

If you struggled to engage with this exercise. Try it a few times. You will find that eventually you will relax into the process.

Before you do the visualisation again, ask yourself the question...
If I *could* see, hear, taste, feel or know what it was like in that coffee shop how would I have experienced it?

Trust – and give it another go. If you still get nothing, don`t worry because your intuition will still gently unfold with the rest of the exercises. We all develop at our own comfortable pace.
Brilliant! – Now you have dipped your toe into the sensory sea of meditation, relaxation, visualisation and with luck you have established which Clair works best for you. As you practice you will find your predominant Clair or Clairs strengthening and your intuitive results becoming more and more accurate. You are now ready to move towards the next exercise.

Chapter 4
The Human Energy Field

All living things are made up of energy and have an energetic field surrounding them. This is sometimes called the aura.

The dictionary definition of the word aura is:

An invisible field of energy or emanation, an atmosphere or feeling that radiates from someone or something.

In Ancient Rome and Ancient Greece, artwork often depicted an aura around people and creatures. In sacred art a glowing halo radiating around the heads of divine beings was common-place in Buddhism, Islam, Christianity and other religions. This could also be the light-emitting lotus depicted at the crown of the head of those considered to have reached spiritual enlightenment in mystical Hindu teachings. In India the energy which flows in and around the body is called prana. In China it is called chi.

The more you practice your relaxation and develop your psychic abilities through the path of intuition, the more likely you are to be able to detect the aura. It is not a given, that you will be able to see auras if this is not your strongest Clair.

We all perceive the energy of others already.
Although, most of us are not always aware of it.
Have your ever been on a crowded tube, in a busy bar, or standing in a queue and felt uncomfortable at the closeness of another person? We generally do not like others invading our personal space. There can be many reasons for this but the main one is subtle. Energetically we are all different. Those with a similar energetic vibration to our own, make us feel less uncomfortable than those whose energy field is totally at odds.

Some believe that we carry our life experience within our aura. All that has happened to us throughout our lifetime is stored within our energetic blueprint which is constantly being modified by our own life journey.

Someone who is compassionate, and caring is most likely at a basic level to be comfortable around people with similar traits.

Like attracts like!

However, the other saying `opposites attract` may be valid. It seems to be that whoever we draw into our orbit, they come in to provide mutual learning and help us advance. By developing your psychic abilities this learning will be speeded up.

How many times have you repeated the same patterns, picked the same type of friends or partners even though your intuition told you it would end in disaster? Once you have upped your psychic skills, you will start to recognise the warning signs and act on them instead of flicking them away in the belief that this time will be different. Your psychic senses will stop you from getting onto the destructive relationship roundabout before you whizz around out of control, fall off and scrape your knees.

Phew! No more bad boys/girls who break your heart, steal your money, damage your self-esteem! *(I`m not bitter!)* Unless of course that floats your boat - then fill your boots.

Chapter 5
Sensing your Own Aura

Before carrying out any of these exercises you need to be relaxed. This creates a more sensitive, perceptive state. Start with the **Breath Balance** meditation you used for the first exercise. Off we go!

- ❖ Regulate your breathing. Start by emptying your lungs. Breathe out fully allowing the exhaled air to make a rushing sound through your mouth.
- ❖ Breathe in deeply through your nose. Hold your breath to a count of 7.
- ❖ Breathe out through your mouth to the count of 8. Repeat until you reach a relaxed state.
- ❖ Imagine any tension leaving the body with each out breath. Imagine calm blissful peace entering the body on the in breath.
- ❖ Using the thumb of your right hand apply light pressure into the palm of your left hand. Rotate the thumb clockwise in a circle at the centre of your palm for a count of 7.
- ❖ Change hands.

- ❖ Using the thumb of your left hand apply light pressure into the palm of your right hand. Rotate the thumb clockwise for a count of 7.
- ❖ Rub your palms together as if you are dusting flour from them.
- ❖ Shake your hands as if you are flicking water from your fingertips for a few seconds.
- ❖ Focus on your breathing.
- ❖ Place your hands in front of you with palms facing but not touching. Start at about 20 – 25cm apart. Gradually move your hands slowly towards each other stopping about 7 to 10 cm apart.
- ❖ Then keeping your palms apart, move your hands from side to side, back and forward, as if you were gently rolling and bouncing an imaginary ball of dough in your hands. Eventually you will feel a subtle resistance between the two hands.
- ❖ If you don`t feel it the first time, then draw your hands apart again and repeat the process a few times.

❖ With eyes closed to help magnify and focus the feelings, play around with sensing your own aura.

❖ Your fingertips are a sensitive point so try bringing the fingertips of each hand closer and closer to those of the other hand without letting them touch.

❖ Take a few deep breaths to keep your self relaxed. Try not to become fixated on an outcome.

With practice, you may feel slight tingling or prickly sensations in your hands or fingers. They may feel hot or cold, some people report feeling as though a feather is tickling the skin. Sometimes you may notice a slight pressure. We are all different, so there is no right or wrong way of receiving energetic information.

Chapter 6
Seeing Your Own Aura

As mentioned earlier we will all have a predominant sense. Not everyone is highly visual. However, this exercise may surprise you. In my experience a dimly lit room works best for seeing your own aura. A perfect time to test this out is lying in bed just before you go off to sleep. Here goes!

- ❖ Regulate your breathing as before. Start by emptying your lungs.
- ❖ Breathe out fully through your mouth.
- ❖ Allow the air to make a rushing sound.
- ❖ Breathe in deeply through your nose. Hold your breath to a count of 7.
- ❖ Breathe out through your mouth. Hold to the count of 8.
- ❖ Repeat until you reach a relaxed state.
- ❖ Imagine any remaining tension leaving the body.
- ❖ Breathe in calm blissful peace.

❖ Stretch your hands out in front of you and carry out the energetic `dough ball` exercise from before to pump up your aura.

❖ Keep your breathing relaxed and slow. Move your hands into a prayer position but don't allow them to touch. Leave a few centimetres gap between them.

❖ Half close your eyes so that you soften your vision. Peer into the space between your palms then move your hands in and out as if you were bouncing the `dough ball` between them.

❖ When you feel any sensation or resistance, pause - making sure you leave a gap. Then soft gaze through the gap in between your hands, resting your vision just beyond.

❖ Continue to keep your breathing rhythmic and slow. You may notice a slight pale glow emanating from your palms.

❖ When you first start doing this it will probably be colourless. However, with practice you may start to see more specific colours.

❖ Now stretch your fingers apart with palms facing you and soft focus between the gaps in your fingers and around the periphery of your hands.

❖ If you don't see anything close to your hands at first, soften your vision even more and allow your gaze to drift further away from your hands.

❖ Effectively, what you are doing is not looking directly at your hands you are looking at the space around them but with an awareness of your hands. Our aura fluctuates in size, yours may not be as tight to the body as you would first imagine.

❖ Now turn your palms away from you and repeat the above.

If you have success with this exercise – try detecting the aura around your bare feet.

This one also works well whilst lying in bed in a dimly lit room.

❖ Place a cushion under your feet to elevate them slightly.

> *Obviously, you won`t be able to do the `dough ball` exercise with your feet (unless you are incredibly talented!)*

❖ If you are relaxed enough, imagine with each out breath you are pushing energy out through your toes into your aura.

Keep practising – if all else fails, it's a creative alternative to counting sheep!

Chapter 7
Sensing the Aura of Others

This one is fun! Seeing, feeling, and knowing all come into play with this exercise.

You will need to have at least one other person to help you carry this out. If you have two or three friends who will explore this with you – even better.

Once again you need a dimly lit room – although not as dark as a night-time bedroom. You can do this in daylight, but the room needs to have curtains or blinds drawn. You also need a white or light un-patterned background wall. Give each participant a pen and paper so they can jot down their findings during the exercise.

❖ **Breath Balance**.
❖ Ask one member of the group, **Person A** to stand just in front of the light background wall with their legs slightly parted and arms spread out to either side.

35

❖ **Person A** needs to slow their breathing. And with each out breath imagine they are pushing bright light out through every cell of their body, *(as an accomplished aura reader this won`t be necessary – but it helps when you are practising)*.

❖ Now you, and any other `aura readers` stand about 2 to 3 metres away from **Person A**. Far enough back so that you can see their entire body and an area of blank wall surrounding them.

❖ Half close your eyes. Soften your vision so you are looking through a slight haze.

❖ Imagine you are looking out through a third eye located slightly above the centre of your eyebrows.

❖ Keep your breathing regulated. Then staying in a detached day-dreamy state start to soft-look at the area surrounding **Person A**.

❖ Start at the head and shoulder area as this seems to emit the strongest reading.

❖ View around the outer edge of the body. Allow the impressions to come.

❖ You may see a vapour-like haze, swirls or patches of colour.

❖ If you are not seeing anything at all ask yourself the question. If I *could* see this aura – what colour and shape would it be?

❖ Take notice of any feelings within your own body as you view **Person A**`s energy field.

❖ Don`t give up too quickly. It takes a while for your eyes to adjust. Or for your third eye to awaken.

❖ Once you have gathered as much information as you can. Pick up your pen and paper and jot down your results. Any colour, any impressions, any feelings, any shapes etc.

❖ For fun, compare notes with the other viewers.

❖ You should quickly discover which Clairs are at work for you. Validation comes when others confirm sensing the same as you did.

❖ You will find that the feelings and impressions that you have picked up as a viewer, often resonate with **Person A**.

❖ At this stage don't become down-hearted if the results weren`t what you expected. You are re-training old `psychic` muscles which have been dormant for a while.

❖ The next step is to have **Person A** imagine they are pushing a specific colour out into their aura – have the aura readers write down what they perceive.

❖ Now try swapping so that each person has a chance to become a reader.

The more you change it around, the more relaxed you will all become. And the greater the results. Keep it light-hearted because laughter also helps to boost the aura. Once you get some good results – a great twist on this exercise is to have **Person A** use their acting skills to imagine different emotional scenarios.

The viewers can then note any changes in aura pattern, colour or shape.

Ask **Person A** to recall a happy, sad, hilarious, scary, dramatic or loving situation from the past, create it in their mind`s eye just as though they were there again. They can either tell you which emotion they are invoking or let you guess from the results.

The one thing all these exercises have in common, is the need to trust and believe in what you receive; before long you will have cracked it! Practice, practice, practice.

Do I glimpse a glowing, vibrant halo emanating from the crown of your head?

Aha...I think I do!

Chapter 8
Sensing the Aura of Other Living Things

We each have a unique energetic blue-print, whether we be animal, mineral or vegetable. Our aura fluctuates in shape and size depending on our mental, emotional, spiritual and physical state.

Next time you are outside in nature, find a tree to observe.

- ❖ Breath Balance.
- ❖ Soft focus your vision around the tips of the branches. See if you can perceive its aura.
- ❖ If you are struggling – squint through half closed eyelids, move your line of sight gradually outwards, moving further from the branch ends. The aura of a tree can be surprisingly vast.
- ❖ It is worth trying this in varying conditions; Full sunshine – evening time - half-light – during a rain shower – before a storm – after a storm.

❖ Try your skills out on all different tree types; Oak, Beech, Silver birch, Conifers, Chestnut, Willow, etc., notice how the auras vary in intensity and how they make you feel.

❖ Note any colour associated with the aura of your chosen tree. Does the colour invoke any emotions or thoughts within you? If so, do you think this reflects anything the tree is experiencing.

If you enjoyed this practice, then you may want to try reading the aura of your family cat, dog or rabbit in the same way.

It is easier to carry out when they are resting peacefully. This way you can take your time. *(Plus, it is pretty challenging trying to read the energy field of a bouncy Labrador chasing a ball!)*

Put yourself into a relaxed state using **Breath Balance** and the soft-focus eye method. The process is remarkably similar to tree reading.
It is possible that your pet will, twitch, fidget, or wake up and move away when you start doing this.

Animals are highly-sensitive to energy fluctuations and will know they are being watched. This is a natural safety tool they have perfected over thousands of years to protect them from predators. But, keep trying. Most domestic cats or dogs will eventually stop waking when they realise that it is you who is watching them and there is no threat.

Chapter 9
Upping Your Animal Magnetism

Imagine you are standing in a packed bar and across the crowded room you catch sight of your future life partner. You instantly recognise the face, body shape and energy of your soul mate. The one you have been waiting for up to this moment in your life. He or she doesn't know it yet. But you do!

What if you were able to use your psychic abilities to draw that person across the room towards you? How cool would that be? Would it be ethical? Maybe. If other factors are at work, and **they** also know that you are their soul mate, and their higher-self or intuition is making contact with you on a subtle level and agreeing that this is the time and place. Then of course that would be ok.

Bring it on I hear you say!

This exercise is a step towards that goal. For this one, you need to be outside in nature again. Should you be fortunate enough to have access to farmland, find yourself a field of grazing cattle or horses. If this is not possible you could try the exercise at a petting zoo or one of the amazing city farms dotted around the country.

- ❖ **Breath Balance** meditation.
- ❖ When you are in a relaxed state begin to gaze softly at the animals in the field. Try to detect their auras. Keep your focus soft.
- ❖ Say a few internal words to reassure the animals – tell them you mean no harm and that you are here to send them some love. *(Nobody is judging you – so please humour me!)*
- ❖ Imagine a shaft of golden liquid light pouring down from above.
  (Depending on your dominant sense you may feel, see, or hear this, if you still have no awareness – simply TRUST that it is occurring).

- ❖ Imagine a pure white lotus flower at the top of your head. Now imagine it`s petals starting to open allowing that shaft of liquid light to pour into its centre and through the top of your head filling your body. Feel the liquid light lifting, re-charging and invigorating you.
- ❖ With each in-breath feel yourself calming.
- ❖ Imagine the liquid energy which is coursing into you trickling into your toes, your feet, legs, torso, neck and head until you are full to the brim.
- ❖ Golden light now spilling over and cascading down the outside of your aura.
- ❖ When you breathe in - pull more golden light into your body.
- ❖ As you breathe out – imagine pushing that vibrant light out through the pores of your skin – as if you were refreshing your aura.
- ❖ Keeping a soft focus – slow breathing and pulling in golden light and pushing it into your energy field.
- ❖ Know that with each out-breath your aura is being pumped up to huge proportions.

❖ This is the fun bit – Mentally call the animals towards you. Imagine you are reeling them in with an imaginary golden string.

❖ With practice you will find them making their way towards you. Pulled in by your `animal magnetism`.

Fabulous – another technique for your psychic backpack!

Once you have perfected this skill – try it with the human animal. A gentle word of warning. If you try this in a packed bar, make sure you are fixated on only one person. Otherwise you could find yourself drowning in a sea of free drinks and persistent admirers!

Hmmm. That one is your call!

Chapter 10
Stepping it Up a Notch
Protecting your Energy Field

This book is geared to honing your intuition to enhance your daily life and decision making. And if you wish to progress to work as a psychic reader or medium then this is a good grounding to get you started.

If we accept that the unseen world exists – then it is logical that within that unseen world there will be both positive and negative energies at work, the same as there are in the seen world. Therefore, if you are serious about carrying out psychic or mediumship readings then you will need to protect your own energy field from anything which is not coming from a place of good intention. Most people need to put protection in place because they are not able to see with their physical eyes when there is negative energy close by. By honing your psychic skills and activating your third-eye centre it helps you to perceive at a different level.

We`ve all seen the movies. Spooky apparitions, dark forces and invisible bogie men, energy vampires and unfriendly ghosts lurking ready to take you over or at the least scare the pants off you! If you are intending to use your psychic abilities to help others, and you are coming from a place of positivity and loving intention, then you should hopefully never encounter anything this dodgy. But….and there is always a but, the more you straddle the seen and unseen worlds to do psychic work at some point you may encounter energies which could knock you out of balance. These can take the form of energy vampires, spirit attachments, negative thought-forms. As your energy field becomes stronger and lighter, you will act a bit like a light bulb in a darkened room attracting moths into your orbit. Some like-minded `moths` will be attracted because of the warm loving glow you give off without creating any issues.

On the rare occasion you may attract a few that want to drain your energy, disempower you and knock you off track.

It is said that even if someone is constantly thinking bad thoughts about you, directing their anger or jealousy towards you, then it can eventually drain your energy. You have probably encountered these negative effects at some time but maybe dismissed them as imagination and muddled on. The effects can manifest in many ways. If any of the following symptoms come on immediately after being around someone who had a negative attitude, then you may have been affected:

- Feeling drained and tired.
- Depression, fear or anxiety with no apparent source.
- Dark thoughts.
- Weepiness.
- Angry feelings.
- A sticky or cobweb feeling in your energy field.
- Nightmares or night terrors.
- Unexplained headaches – neck and shoulder pain.
- Nausea or sickness.

(of course, these symptoms could be due to an underlying health issue - always check with a medical practitioner if these feelings persist)

The best way to avoid this is to be prepared and put some psychic protection in place. The plus side of protecting your energy field is that it will make you feel more empowered and positive regardless of whether you intend to use your abilities in everyday life, relationships, business or for carrying out readings. Based on my own awareness of the spirit world I have a belief in spirit guides and guardian angels. I know they move around us at all times. But I also believe that we are on the earth plane to learn and grow. Unless we specifically ask our guides or angels to intervene, to assist us on our journey then they will stay firmly in the background. They are happy to step up and assist when we ask.

There are many different forms of spirit guides working on multiple levels and dimensions.
Granny or Uncle Bert who has passed away but had a special bond with us during life can pop in and out to help us make decisions and stay safe.

Then there are higher level beings who may have lived on the earth plane in the past, wise spiritual beings with a higher vibration who may help us in our work. If you choose to become a psychic reader, medium or spiritual healer then these spirit guides can make themselves known and assist you in making the right choices. If you are keen to save the planet and concerned about global healing, then you may encounter nature spirits and elementals who work with you.

For me, the presence of angelic beings has always been a given. I call on the angelic realm to keep my vibration as high and clear as it can be. The simplest method of Psychic Protection is to call in the Angels of Protection. Archangel Michael is often depicted carrying a sword and shield.

You can make up your own little mantra to call him in – it needn`t be complicated. Make your intention clear and Archangel Michael will do the rest. An example of a protection mantra could be:

I call upon my guides and Angels.
I call upon Archangel Michael and the angels of protection.
Surround me with the highest vibration of love, peace and light.

Place me in a bubble of angelic protection – wrap your wings around me, filter out any unwanted energies which are not for my highest good.
Allow only positive energies into my orbit. It is done.

Create your own protection prayer or mantra that fits comfortably with your own belief system. There are other methods believed to be effective in invoking a shield around you while you work. Some imagine a vibrant royal blue cloak being wrapped around their shoulders and covering the crown of their head. Others imagine an impermeable bubble surrounding them. Others ask for their guides to do the work for them. If you believe in the spirit world and psychic abilities, then this will not feel alien to you. Thought is simply another form of energy so by using all your senses to feel, see and trust that protection is in place, then so it shall be!

Crystals have been used for millennia to enhance spiritual perception, for healing and in amulet form for protection against negative influence. Crystals and gemstones are known to alter, repair, heal and re-balance the body`s vibrational resonance.

We cannot be sure how the ancients Egyptians, Chinese, Romans, Greeks knew about the healing and protective properties of gemstones, but they seemed instinctively drawn to utilise them in balancing their mind body and spirits. The bonus is they are beautiful to wear too. Find yourself a protective stone to carry about your person. Here are a few suggestions, known to be effective:

Black obsidian - Apache Tear - Black Tourmaline Smokey Quartz – Tigers Eye - Labradorite – Amethyst.

These are all known to be great for protection. Take yourself to a crystal shop and choose your own. That way you will find the right one for you. With your new heightened sensitivity, you will soon work out which crystals resonate with your own energetic make up.

A simple test is to place your chosen gemstone in the palm of your hand.

- ❖ Close your eyes and relax.
- ❖ Check out any sensations in your body and thoughts or feelings.

- ❖ If you feel uplifted, then that is a good sign.
- ❖ If you feel unsettled or nauseous then choose a different type of gemstone. Your intuition will lead you to the right one for you!

There are many ways of protecting your own space. It is worth doing some more research to find a method which feels comfortable for you.

If you should feel the need to cleanse your energy field of any unwanted negativity, a relaxing soak in a sea-salt, rock-salt or Epsom salt bath is one of the most effective methods of cleansing your aura. A mug full of salt is about the right amount with a few drops of essential oil added to the bath water to create a more uplifting experience. For me, a maximum of 15 – 20 minutes soak is enough, any longer and you may start to feel drained.

Chapter 11
Creating your Sacred Space

Now you are stepping it up and you have your protection in place. I would advise creating a `sacred space` to carry out your exercises and beyond that, to do readings for others.

The reason for having a specific zone or area for this work is it means you can create a vibe which is comfortable for you, one where you can control your environment and external vibrational interference can be kept to a minimum. This way you will feel safer and when you tune in to your psychic abilities you will be able to perceive your messages much more clearly. Also, if you have a familiar energy around you, then all your psychic impressions will be stronger. It`s a bit like having your own bedroom to retreat to when you go to sleep, a place you can trust at a time when you are at your most vulnerable. Your sacred space serves the same purpose. As you become more accomplished in using your psychic powers then you will learn how to *open up* and *close down* when you are in surroundings which are less under your control.

To lift the energy and cleanse your sacred space you could also burn sage smudge sticks in that area. They are available from most holistic or mind, body, spirit outlets. Originally used by the Native Americans to drive out unwanted spirits it is believed that the smoke from the sage wraps itself around any negativity and carries it out of an open door or window. You can also smudge your own energy field if you are feeling under par or affected after a reading.

Once you have lit the smudge stick you then blow out any flames leaving it smouldering. Sage emits thick plumes of fragrant smoke. Pass the smudge stick from hand to hand encircling your aura working from the top of your body down to your feet. If you have someone else who can do this for you it is obviously easier.

A word of warning – smouldering sage can drop hot ash so take care around your hair, clothing, carpets etc.

Traditionally the Native Americans used an abalone seashell into which they placed the lit sage this would be held in the palm of their hand.

The other hand would hold a feather which was used to waft the smoke in all directions.

If you can't get your hands on an abalone shell, then a saucepan to catch any sparks works well. A magazine or hand-held fan could replace the feather! Anything suitable for wafting. Not so spiritual but equally as effective!!

Your sacred space needs to be calm and peaceful. It is better if you have no electronic appliances in this space to keep intruding vibes at bay. Surround yourself with images which give you comfort. Maybe invest in a Himalayan salt lamp or candle holder. Salt is a great cleanser of negative energy – in the same way as you feel uplifted and clear when walking by the sea, a salt lamp will purify your surroundings before, during and after your readings.

Introducing crystals into your space is a clever idea. Crystals such as amethyst, lapis lazuli or clear quartz are particularly good for helping stimulate your `third eye` and promoting psychic vision. Rose Quartz creates a loving peaceful environment.

Blue lace agate, celestite or turquoise are all good for helping you to communicate well.

If you investigate the properties of the different gemstones, then you will quickly be drawn to the ones which will create the type of working environment you desire.

Brilliant! – Now you have your own sacred space.

Burn some incense or scented candles to create the perfect mood for your psychic work. Breathe in the scent of pure potential!

Chapter 12
Creating a Symbolism Journal

Because we each perceive our psychic input differently, one of the things I would recommend, is to create your own symbolism journal. Buy yourself a special journal specifically for this use. Get one that stands alone from any of your other notebooks. It doesn`t need to be expensive, some of the charity shops do fabulous ones created on recycled paper. This little book is your gateway to working with the psychic world, so it should be special. Mine was given to me by a friend it is beautifully bound and has a little bronze lock on it. Make yours significant and special. The twinklier the better I say!

If you are a prolific dreamer and you remember your dreams on waking, then it is always good to write them down the minute you open your eyes. Have a notepad beside your bed so that you can make jottings before your conscious mind becomes too active.

We tend to dream in symbolism, and I am sure you have seen many books on dream interpretation on the shelves of bookshops.

These can be helpful if you have not developed your intuition or psychic abilities yet. But I feel it is more advantageous to decipher your own dreams.

If animals creep into your dreams. Ask yourself what aspect of your life they may represent. Accept the first impression that comes to you and make a note. For example: if you often dream of birds, how do you feel about them? Do you feel liberated when you see them flying overhead? Are you fearful of them? Do you think of them as representing some kind of omen? What type of bird are you dreaming of? An eagle? A swan? A crow?

Make a note of what they represent to you and add it to your symbolism journal. As you advance you may find yourself needing to modify the meanings of what you see, feel or perceive. This is normal and is a natural part of your development. Eventually you will create an exclusive inner decoding system. It takes a while, but to me, I found it as satisfying as learning a new language.

For example: Daffodils may represent the time frame of spring or the month of March to you; alternatively, they may represent someone from Wales or someone with a sunny disposition. They may remind you of an old aunt **you** adored, who loved daffodils. Whilst doing readings for others, that of course may translate as an old aunt who **they** loved, wishing to pass a message through you.

Once you set the intention that a certain symbol – has a specific meaning then messages will become easier for you to translate. Do you get the idea? If you are drawn towards mediumship you may find, that by saying to the person you are reading for: I see a daffodil. It may have a different significance for them. Don't try to make something fit. If it doesn't make sense to the other person at that moment, it may do later when they have time to dwell on it.

Each reading you do – will give you more validation about how you perceive and receive information. Modify your symbolism journal accordingly.

If you find that you have misinterpreted a symbol add the modification and its latest information to help you build up an accurate database.

Imagine you are doing a reading for someone you have never met.

Set the intention that you can create your own symbolism – not simply what spirit struggles to have you understand.

This helps you receive in your own psychic language rather than that of the sender.

❖ Close your eyes
❖ **Breath Balance**
❖ Do your protection ritual and preparation.
❖ Focus on bringing light down through the crown of your head.
❖ Feel your third eye centre (the point between the middle of your eyebrows) projecting out a stream of colour, then ask for your own unique symbolic imagery for the following:

1.   Marriage
2.   Financial security
3.   Love
4.   Divorce

5.   Separation
6.   Infidelity
7.   Pregnancy
8.   Teenage pregnancy
9.   Miscarriage
10.   Vacation
11.   Alcohol
12.   World travel
13.   Musician
14.   Composer
15.   Author
16.   Poet
17.   Dangerous Sports
18.   Poor eyesight
19.   Paris
20.   Bulimia
21.   Depression
22.   Wealthy
23.   Celebrity
24.   Car mechanic
25.   Control Freak
26.   Healer
27.   Empath
28.   Sensitive
29.   Past
30.   Future

31. In 3 years
32. In 3 months
33. In 3 days
34. Next summer
35. Last summer
36. Summer 1945
37. Spring
38. London
39. Christmas
40. Halloween
41. Silver Anniversary
42. Surprise
43. Christening
44. Twins
45. Celebration
46. Study
47. New career
48. Friendship

Keep adding random words for fun, then check in to see what symbolism emerges for you.

Of course, you may not need to add symbolism for the above if you already have this type of information streamed to you clearly.

This exercise is designed to flex the psychic muscles to give you surety when you pass on your information. Keep practising, practising, practising. The purpose of this psychic workout is to make you, the best you can be!

Remember six gym sessions don't build a six pack!

Chapter 13
News Predictions

This is another enjoyable exercise to stretch your abilities. It takes practice but is worth the effort.

Cut the heading banner from a daily newspaper. The visual aspect of creating a physical representation of a newspaper will help to stimulate your psychic attunement. Glue the heading to the top of a blank sheet of paper, scan and make some copies. Set a time when you won`t be disturbed and set the intention that you are going to predict future news.

- ❖ **Breath Balance**
- ❖ Call upon your spirit guides and ask them for assistance.
- ❖ Put protection in place.
- ❖ A few seconds before you close your eyes to receive – stare at the blank newspaper page – take a few deep breaths and then allow the images to come.

❖ Once you become more adept at this exercise – you may not need to close your eyes.

❖ If you soft-focus your vision you will soon be able to carry this out in a totally relaxed state with eyes open.

❖ Allow the images to sweep (from whichever side you consider to be the past, through your head and out to the side you consider future).

❖ Now visualise those images, words, symbols, events, shapes, colours, aromas etc., landing on your blank page.

Don't worry that you need to put the information down straight away, because you will remember what is relevant.

If it won`t break your focus, you can speak what you are seeing into a voice recorder and write it onto your blank sheet when you have finished seeing/perceiving.

Use whichever technique works best for you.

Do not judge what you receive – record it and trust.

When you have done this for a few days – start checking news reports to see if you have predicted anything correctly, or if there are any similarities in your predictions. Make a record of the date you did your predictions. This is a wonderful way of learning to judge time-scales, which is one of the hardest things for a psychic/medium to interpret accurately.

Good luck and enjoy! Now you have a legitimate reason for obsessing over that rather scrummy newsreader on News at Ten!

Chapter 14
Psychometry

The dictionary definition of psychometry is:
A psychic ability to gather information through the senses about the history of a person by touching/holding an inanimate object belonging to them.

Psychometry is a powerful method of carrying out psychic readings or gathering information. All things animate or inanimate carry a vibration. Objects which have been close to the human aura or worn against the human skin seem to absorb a memory from the wearer. Strong emotional experience, past actions, and even environments from the wearer`s history become stored within the object in the form of vibration. With your psychic perception becoming daily strengthened, psychometry is a really helpful tool.

For this exercise ask a friend to bring you an old object, of which they know the history. If they are a close friend, it may be worth asking them to borrow an object from someone else that you don't know.

This way you will help eliminate the conscious mind scooping up memories you may have retained subliminally. Watches, pieces of jewellery, keys or personal items used on a daily basis are the best because they will be super-charged with emotion. Old diaries and favourite books seem to work well. If you are particularly sensitive and empathic be prepared for an emotional roller-coaster ride. It is worth asking your spirit guides to pass on the impressions for you without the full-blown emotional onslaught. This sounds dramatic – but I had an experience many years ago when I ran a holistic centre. It was the birthday of one of my regular customers, a very spiritual lady. Her husband came in to buy her a gift and made it clear that he was a complete sceptic with regards to anything paranormal. But to test my authenticity he had brought with him a few old items. Would I mind telling him the history of them using psychometry? I felt he was a total non-believer who wanted to debunk anything associated with psychic abilities. But because I wanted to support his wife, I took the objects to the back room, sat quietly and tuned into them.

One item was a small piece of leather strap. I was instantly transported to the WW1 battlefields in Belgium – I could hear the pitiful cries for help from the wounded and dying. I was given a name, a regiment and told that the piece of leather was from an officer`s shoulder strap. He told me how he died – it was heart-rending. He also told me that his brother perished in the same battle. I reported back to the sceptical husband – who turned out to be a university lecturer. I handed him a piece of paper with my findings, he told me the regiment I had mentioned did not have shoulder straps like that and he left. I felt physically and emotionally shaken by the whole experience of witnessing something so strongly, as if I had been there on that battlefield. I also felt hurt because he had given me no feedback. A few days later he returned with one of his students in tow. He had come to tell me that they had carried out some research. He showed me a photo of a war grave with the name and battalion I had given and the location of death as I had told it. He also confirmed that officers in that unit did in fact wear shoulder straps like the one he had shown me.

I like to believe that he now has a more open mind about such things. Psychometry is one of the most powerful forms of accessing your psychic abilities.

Now it's your turn!

- ❖ Put your protection in place.
- ❖ **Breath Balance**.
- ❖ Activate your third eye point located slightly above the inner ends of your eyebrows. You can use your fingertip to locate the slight indent at this point and apply gentle pressure for a few seconds.
- ❖ Sandwich the psychometry item between your palms.
- ❖ Keeping your breathing rhythmic and relaxed. Use one hand to scan the energy of the item, as if you were feeling its aura.
- ❖ Close your eyes if you wish. This helps remove external stimuli and also lessens the likelihood of your conscious mind kicking in.
- ❖ Allow the impressions to filter through.
- ❖ What emotions are you feeling? Do you feel any physical sensations? A stiffness in your limbs, an ache in your heart etc.

❖ Does a person come to mind? If so, allow the perceptions to evolve. Listen, watch, observe, notice any tastes or odours.

❖ Allow a picture to build up of who may have owned the item.

❖ What their life was like?

❖ Do not overanalyse – accept whatever you receive as accurate on some level.

❖ It is always worth remembering that an object may have had more than one owner, so if conflicting information comes through to you, do not dismiss it. For example: you may feel a female presence associated, but also a male. You could receive young energy and older. This could be more than one person.

❖ Make a note after the session. Or if it doesn't bring you to alertness, talk aloud to your friend so that they can make notes for you.

❖ Bring yourself back to full awareness when you feel that all the information has been given.

❖ Ground yourself fully by stamping your feet or rubbing your hands together.

- ❖ Gather your feedback. Be aware that more information will probably filter through over the coming weeks.
- ❖ Hand back the item – flick your fingers as if shaking water from them to separate from the energy of the psychometry piece.

I always wash my hands after a session – it helps to disconnect you from the reading.

You could try this technique at a car boot sale - pick up random items and feel their vibe. It`s probably best not to come straight out with your findings without permission from the owner as that is a bit intrusive. But you could ask what the history of the item is and see if they are happy to oblige. It`s good to try these techniques in varying surroundings. Try an antique shop – you may be able to get some validation there too.

Great stuff – you are moving back to your natural state - a Psychic Superstar!

Chapter 15
Photo Psychometry

Using the same method as the previous exercise – ask a family member or friend to place an old photograph into a non-transparent envelope.

- ❖ Protection
- ❖ **Breath Balance**
- ❖ Soft focus – feel the vibe!
- ❖ Activate your third eye centre by using gentle fingertip pressure for a few seconds. You may feel a tingling sensation as it starts to awaken.
- ❖ Imagine a beam of rich indigo blue light streaming from your forehead like a search- light and resting on the sealed envelope.
- ❖ Close your physical eyes.
- ❖ Imagine using your third eye search-light to scan back and forth across the envelope. Know that this has created an energetic pathway for the information associated with your photograph to make its way into your awareness.

- ❖ Keep your breathing rhythmic and regulated.
- ❖ Imagine a movie screen inside your forehead.
- ❖ See, feel, hear, know, trust that the content of the photograph will be projected onto this movie screen.
- ❖ When you feel you have gathered your information, bring yourself back to full awareness.
- ❖ Give your results. Then – the big reveal. Open the envelope and see how much of what you picked up is accurate.

Well done! Could it be time to start working on a new professional handle? – Mystic Mimi or Psychic Sebastian? Go for something mega exotic to suit your newly unearthed talent!

Chapter 16
Mood Pictures

Ask a friend to cut some pictures from a magazine or print them off the internet. You are looking for a range of subjects that illicit strong emotions. These could be anything like:

A firefighter, a rock guitarist, Stonehenge, the Grand Canyon, a puppy, a spiritual leader. Images to represent; hot, cold, scared, sexy, spiritual, musical, peaceful, etc.

Have your friend place the pictures one by one face down on the table in front of you. Time to use your new-found psychometry skills.

- ❖ Close your eyes.
- ❖ **Breath Balance**.
- ❖ Place your palm over the reverse side of the picture.
- ❖ Allow any impressions to come in.
- ❖ Take note of feelings within your body.
- ❖ Does the picture make you feel sad, happy, hot, cold etc.

❖ Allow any sounds, odours, images, feelings or knowing to come forward.

❖ Take notice if any internal symbolism which you have created previously pops up.

❖ Tell your friend exactly what you pick up.

❖ Move on to the next picture. The more you do this – the easier it will become.

What can I say? Another step towards psychic awesomeness!

Chapter 17
Name Psychometry

This exercise is a slight twist on the normal methods of psychometry which usually involves holding a piece of jewellery, keys, or personal items with a view to unleashing the memories stored within that item. Gather together a few willing friends.

- ❖ Put protection in place.
- ❖ Eyes closed.
- ❖ **Breath Balance** – at this stage you could talk your group through this relaxation method if they are receptive to it.
- ❖ Eyes open.
- ❖ Keep your breathing relaxed and rhythmic.
- ❖ Each person in the group should print or sign their name onto a piece of paper.
- ❖ Fold the paper so that the names cannot be seen.

- ❖ Ask each participant to place their folded paper against their body at the solar plexus. This is the energy centre located just below your rib cage, between the centre of your chest and your tummy button.
- ❖ **Breath Balance**
- ❖ Each person should imagine their energy, feelings, thoughts, being infused into the paper.
- ❖ Gather up the papers and pop them into a bowl in the centre of the room where everyone can see them.
- ❖ You can either take turns to do this psychic exercise - or if you feel confident and really want to impress your friends then take one of the pieces of paper from the bowl – don`t peek inside.
- ❖ Close your eyes again.
- ❖ Regulate your breathing and hold the paper between your palms. You are now tuning in to the energy of the person whose name is written inside.

❖ As you breathe in and out sense any impressions, thoughts, feelings, smells, sounds, words which come to you.

❖ Gently press the spot between your brows with a fingertip for about 30 - 45 seconds then hold the paper to your third eye point. This helps to stimulate insight and awareness.

❖ Feel your third eye becoming activated, imagine it blinking. Trust that it is opening and in the same way that physical eyes work, imagine you are looking out directly from your third eye scanning the paper and absorbing the named person`s thoughts and impressions infused within.

❖ As you do this imagine a beam of rich indigo blue light streaming like a search-light from your third eye point. This will act as an energetic pathway.

❖ You may wish to hold the paper to your own solar plexus, this works particularly well if your predominant Clair is clairsentience.

❖ This should be cheerful and fun. So be thoughtful when relaying your impressions.

❖ Ask yourself some questions as you tune into the energy from the paper.

❖ Are you feeling hot or cold?

❖ Is this person shy or an extrovert?

❖ What is their mood? Are they happy or sad? Tired or excitable?

❖ What is the predominant emotion working through this person's life at present?

❖ Take note of any colours, scenes, feelings.

❖ Allow the information to come but try not to fixate too strongly on anything you receive, or your conscious mind will go into analytical mode.

❖ The idea is for the impressions to come towards you as if they were on a slow-moving conveyor belt. Try to acknowledge them then let them move away.

❖ You may find it easier to talk out loud as you receive the impressions, or you may prefer to wait until you have gathered what you need.

❖ If you received a strong feeling of who this paper belonged to the moment you touched it, it is still better to give the group what you have picked up before announcing who you think it is.

❖ Open the paper and show the group.

If you are wrong with your name guess – do not worry, it does take practice.

Ask the person whose name **is** on the slip, if any of the feelings or impressions fit them, even if you gave the wrong name. You can be incredibly accurate with this test. In the early days of practice, it is easy for our conscious mind to kick in when we have to say whose name we think is written down. This is especially true when we know the events which have been going on around certain people.

Practice – practice – practice.

Chapter 18
Crystal Psychometry

The previous exercise for name psychometry can also be done using crystal gemstones.

Gather together a group of friends. Have a tray scattered with gemstones of varying types and colours in the centre of your group. Make sure they are all completely different so that they can be recognised again after the session.

Cleanse the gemstones before use. This is important because they are known to absorb energy from their environment, hence the need to be purified. This can be done by standing them in a bowl of rock or sea salt for a few hours. Popping them out into the bright sunlight for an hour or two, leaving them overnight outside in the full moonlight, rinsing them in a fast running stream, rinsing them in the sea, or passing them through the smoke of an incense stick or sage smudge stick.

Now you are ready to begin.

❖ **Breath Balance.**

❖ Ask your friends to take one gemstone each from the tray whilst you keep your eyes closed or leave the room.

❖ Any unchosen gemstones need to be removed from the tray and placed to one side.

❖ Each person then holds their chosen crystal to their third eye or solar plexus and breathes their energy, thoughts and feelings into it, as previously for the name psychometry. It is worth taking a little time over this part.

❖ Then, still unseen by you they must place their gemstone back on the tray.

❖ Using your psychic tuning in methods, read the energy of each gemstone giving feedback of what you have picked up.

❖ If you wish to make a bold suggestion as to whose gemstone it was, then do so.

❖ Move onto the next gemstone. Repeat the process.

❖ Even if you give the name of the person you believe infused the gemstone it may be worth asking your participants not to comment until you have finished reading all the crystals. Otherwise as the odds narrow down you may be swayed towards guesswork.

❖ Once finished, ask if your impressions were accurate.

Are you surprised at the results?

Don`t doubt your abilities if you weren`t 100% accurate. Even people who use their psychic sensitivity frequently don't get a perfect hit rate. Your environment, the company you are keeping, your conscious mind and `making a lulu of yourself` insecurities, can all sway results. Try saying some positive affirmations before and after every practice to boost belief and change the hard wiring of any negative thoughts. Words carry powerful energy. If you say something enough times with conviction; feeling the words as though they had already happened, then it alters your vibration and directs you towards a positive result.

This is good daily practice even when you are not doing readings. Positive affirmations create a much happier psychological state and improve your well-being.

Here are some suggestions:

My perceptions are clear and correct.
My third eye is aligned and accurate.
I am attuned to my sixth sense.
My intuition guides me safely.
I trust the messages my senses provide.
My awareness is heightened and accurate.
My intuition guides me towards the correct choices.
I trust my intuition.
My psychic awareness is accurate.
I safely unleash my inner psychic.
I make the right choices by trusting my instincts.
I am happy, successful, abundant, joyful, healthy and loved.

You get the idea. Give it a go, do it frequently but always choose positive, uplifting, empowering words. Smiling while you say your affirmations releases endorphins, ups the feel-good factor and magnifies the result.

Of course, if you do this while you are sat on the train on your commute – be prepared for a few strange looks and a flurry of seat shifting away from the person with the manic grin!

Chapter 19
Crystal Readings

You only need one other person to help you with this one. Collect a selection of different gemstones, try to include a variety of colours up to a maximum of about 20. Cleanse them of any external energies using one of the methods from the previous exercise. Find a little drawstring bag to put them in. Spend some time familiarising yourself with each gemstone prior to this reading. Take time to hold each one and create an idea of what the colours represent to you. How do they make you feel? What do they symbolise?

For example: Pink rose quartz is usually associated with love, babies, the feminine, matters of the heart, relationships.

Purple amethyst is often associated with healing physical ailments, expelling nightmares, aiding psychic and spiritual growth. Brown and gold tigers-eye is used for protection, it releases fear and anxiety, helps you to feel secure and stable.

❖ Ask your friend to hold the bag and shake it gently.

❖ Suggest they close their eyes, take a few deep breaths and withdraw 3 gemstones from the bag.

❖ Place the first chosen gemstone in front of you on the table.

❖ Place the second chosen gemstone to its right.

❖ And the third to the second stone`s right.

❖ *Stone 1* represents the person`s recent past.

❖ *Stone 2* represents the present.

❖ *Stone 3* represents the near future.

❖ Tune into the gemstones, look at the relationship between all three crystals. Allow any feelings and images to come to you.

❖ You may wish to refer to a crystal meaning book to start you off and to help you get an idea of what messages are coming through.

❖ *With time you will have your own understanding of the meanings, which will grow with practice. Always trust your own interpretation - it will be correct on some level. You will be surprised how accurate these readings can be.*

❖ If your friend has a specific question, ask them to pick between one and five crystals for you to interpret.

❖ These can be read one by one or grouped together, look at the relationship between the gemstones and you will feel a story unfolding.

❖ If you remain relaxed during this process you will be able to receive clear information to pass on and it will help you to detach from the outcome.

Well done! Keep practising this one, it is really rewarding when you are able to help someone gain clarity over a matter. Eventually, you will be proficient enough to do readings for people you don`t know already, if that appeals. But always remember to be truthful, be compassionate, and be kind.

The most important aspect of doing readings for another is to leave them feeling upbeat, positive and healed. Once you have honed your psychic skills you are in a privileged position. Keep your findings between you and the person you are reading for. It is up to them to share if they wish.

Never use this ability in a controlling or negative way.

Unless of course the person you are reading for is your tyrannical boss – then I suppose, anything goes!

Chapter 20
Psychic Ink Splodges

Here is a chance to try an exercise with intuition prompts. Did you ever create ink blot pictures when you were a child? You will need a piece of A4 paper and a bottle of ink, or you can use kids' poster paints. Make a vertical fold down the centre of the page. Blob a few drops of ink along the gulley of the fold. Then carefully fold the right and left sides together. Place your sheet of folded paper on the table in front of you and using your fingers spread the ink within to create a pattern. Unfold the sheet, you will have a random but symmetrical pattern.

- ❖ **Breath Balance**.
- ❖ Put your protection in place.
- ❖ When you feel peaceful and centred then ask your higher-self/your sub-conscious mind or your guides to give you some valid insight. Something you need to know or understand.
- ❖ Soften the focus of your vision and peer gently at your ink splodge. You will notice pictures forming within the pattern.

❖ Say aloud what you see.

❖ Take it further, keep yourself as relaxed as possible and ask: Why am I seeing this image or symbol? What does it mean to me? For example: If you see a butterfly, you may have a connection with butterflies which means something extremely specific to you or it could be that you see them as a symbol of transformation, of rebirth, of new beginnings, of breaking free, of spreading your wings, freedom.

❖ Allow the images and symbolic meanings to come. Trust that your first thought is valid. Try not to let your logical mind take over.

❖ If you find your mind drifting away from your reading, it may be that you are unconsciously avoiding the message, or your logical mind may be trying to take back control.

❖ Should this happen, slow down your breathing, look away from the image for a few seconds. Then repeat your relaxation method and start fresh.

❖ It works in the same way as old-fashioned tea leaf readings. The reader would lose themselves in the shapes and interpret them.

❖ If you initially struggle to decipher your ink splodges, you may find it helpful to obtain a book on signs and symbols to start you off.

❖ Eventually you will be able to create your own symbolism which is unique to you and you can add them to your symbol journal.

It will become easier the more you practice. It won`t be long before you are a master at reading the content. You will be astounded at the accuracy of your predictions. Try doing this for your friends. Ask them to create an ink splodge. Tell them what you see. Allow them to tell you if the symbol you have given resonates. Does it mean anything to them? If **you** feel strongly about its meaning, then with their permission start to interpret in more detail.

Do not let your ego take over.

If your interpretation means nothing to them – then suggest they make a note of what you have said and let you know in the future if anything materialises relating to your reading. It is helpful for you to have validation when you do get things right. But do not be despondent if nothing seems to fit for them. It is quite common for a person to mention in passing sometime later that what you saw was accurate. Do not let it knock your confidence. On some level what you see is always correct. It may be that the timing is out.

If the idea of creating your own ink splodges is too messy, then there are pre-made cards that you can buy.

Once you have perfected ink splodge reading – you could always sign your masterpiece and give it as a souvenir to those you do your readings for. It may be worth a fortune one day.

Have fun Picasso!

Chapter 21
Scrying

The dictionary definition of scrying is:

A form of divination where you peer at or into a reflective surface, or suitable medium to receive images for prophecy or guidance. It is believed to have originated from the word `descry` to discover or detect something.

In Ancient times divination would be carried out by the chosen few as it was considered a gift from the divine, these were the priests, seers, augurers and the Druids.

The great French visionary Nostradamus is said to have gained insight through gazing into a magic mirror but also through hydromancy - scrying with water. So here we go – it`s your turn!

You will need a bowl *(I use a Tibetan singing bowl and it works perfectly but any bowl either metal, glass or china will do.)* Some dark coloured ink or food colouring, a candle or candles. Fill your bowl almost to the top with water.

Colour with a few drops of the ink or food colouring - keep adding the colouring until you are either unable to see the bottom of the bowl or the colouring creates cloud-like patterns. If you try one method and struggle to get results – then try the other way. Place your lit candle or candles far enough away from the bowl that you won`t burn yourself or catch your hair on them when you are scrying – it kills the mood!

- ❖ Put your protection in place.
- ❖ Set the intention for which type of information you wish to receive: i.e. personal guidance or prophecy.
- ❖ **Breath Balance**
- ❖ Soften your gaze.
- ❖ If using the fully coloured water method, disturb the water slightly with a pencil to create ripples.
- ❖ Allow the images and impressions to come.
- ❖ If using the method with splashes of ink on the water, you may find yourself drawn to reading the ink spots or the spaces between.

❖ Make some notes of your results including the date. Look back at these from time to time to check how accurate you were.

Great – You can now set yourself up in a corner of your favourite coffee shop and scry your cappuccino!

Chapter 22
Aeromancy – Cloud reading

In Ancient Rome and Greece, it was believed that the gods controlled the weather; how the weather was behaving was considered a reflection of the mood of the gods. Aeromancy is the art of reading the weather, particularly scrying within cloud formations.

Following the same principles as all other methods of scrying, cloud reading can be particularly satisfying. It has the added advantage of taking you out into nature and the benefits associated with connecting with the planet. Scrying can create a deeper understanding of your psychic abilities.

It is worth practising regularly – cloud reading can be done easily without onlookers thinking you a bit strange. Pop on your sunnies, lay out on the grass in your garden or local park on a warm day and up your psychic perception whilst soaking up that vitamin D.

The combination of slow regulated breathing and soft focusing your vision helps to remove mind chit-chat and unhelpful thoughts too.

A great de-stresser for the lunch break.

Chapter 23
Pyromancy – Fire Gazing

How often have you found yourself lost in the images licking upwards from the embers of a blazing fire - disappearing into a fantasy world of dancing goblins and fire nymphs? Okay – only me then! Well if you have never tried it you don`t know what you are missing. It is truly magical. Fire-watching seems to stir something primitive and comforting deep within.

Divination by gazing into the crackling flames in a fireplace, campfire or a single candle flame is known as pyromancy.

You can carry this exercise out for yourself or for another. If you are searching for the answer to a question and seem to be unable to access your higher self or intuition – this is a great method to bring clarity.

- ❖ Put protection in place.
- ❖ Pose the question you want answered.
- ❖ **Breath Balance**.
- ❖ Soften your vision.
- ❖ Peer into the flames.

❖ What do you see? What feelings do the images illicit within you?

❖ Notice any obvious shapes or symbols.

❖ Interpret your results. Jot them down and date them.

❖ Try gazing into a candle flame, this is particularly powerful when communicating with spirit.

❖ If you have a spirit who is trying hard to make contact, but the messages are blurry or weak, suggest they use the candle flame for yes/no answers.

❖ Ask a question and wait for the response.

❖ If you are indoors, it is preferable to work in a darkened room where you will not be distracted by other forms of lighting.

❖ Disconnect from the conversation by saying something like: *Goodbye, thank you, this communication is now closed.*

❖ Turn on the light, clap your hands, go out into the fresh air for a few moments, or stamp your feet to ground yourself fully.

Jot down your results. Review them over a cuppa and a biscuit.

Now you are sizzling!

Chapter 24
Ceromancy – Candle wax divination

Back as far as the time of the Ancient Celts ceromancy was practiced in order to gain insight and foretell the future. Melted wax formations from a free-standing candle would be observed and interpreted. This could be by way of reading the wax drips or by purposely tilting the melting candle over a bowl of water. The wax solidifies when it makes contact with the water – giving the reader shapes and symbols to focus on for guidance. Why not give this one a go? Use the same methods as the previous exercises:

- ❖ Put protection in place.
- ❖ **Breath Balance.**
- ❖ Soften vision.
- ❖ Allow the psychic messages to flood in.
- ❖ Ground and disconnect.
- ❖ Record and date your results.

Eureka! You are rather good at this lark!

Chapter 25
Crystallomancy - Crystal Ball Scrying

I find this is one of the most effective and exciting forms of scrying used in many ancient civilisations.

Choose a clear crystal to work with it can be either a ball or a crystal point. You may prefer to choose a clear quartz rock crystal, the naturally occurring inclusions can help to illicit powerful visual psychic stimulation. Alternatively, you may prefer to use a perfectly clear manufactured lead crystal ball.

Before you start - cleanse your crystal ball/point to remove any residues which it may have absorbed. This will give you the purest most accurate reading. You can cleanse your crystal by placing it into a bowl of sea or rock salt for a few hours, popping it out into the full moonlight/sunlight, smudging around it with a sage stick, putting it into running water or any other method which works for you.

When you are ready to start, take yourself to a darkened room and light a couple of candles to set the mood.

- ❖ Put your protection in place.
- ❖ **Breath Balance**.
- ❖ Soften your vision.
- ❖ Allow yourself to relax enough so that you slip into a slightly altered state.
- ❖ The first thing that usually occurs is a hazy mist appears within your crystal.
- ❖ Keep your vision soft.
- ❖ If you have a question you would like answered then be clear, ask your question.
- ❖ Be patient.
- ❖ See what appears. Try to allow the images or feelings to come before giving up and disconnecting.
- ❖ It is normal to feel apprehensive as you start to get results. Keep your breathing regulated and remind yourself that your guides are with you.
- ❖ Eventually you will start to find a story unfolding.

❖ Persevere until you feel you have received what you need.

❖ Jot down your results.

❖ Sometimes the meanings will make sense instantly, occasionally you will receive your impressions after you have detached from the session.

❖ Ground yourself and pat yourself on the back.

Result! Can you feel it? Your psychic muscles are throbbing.

Next step dangly gold earrings and a tent at the end of the pier!

Chapter 26
Runic symbols

The origin of rune stones is shrouded in mystery. In old Norse the meaning of the word rune translates roughly as secret wisdom and knowledge and seems to be entwined with Norse mythology. The Norse god, Odin, was believed by the Vikings to have created the runes. Myth tells that he attached himself to the Yggdrasil tree (a huge Ash tree, whose branches stretch up above the heavens) in the hope that he would absorb some of its secrets to pass on to his people.

Many cultures have used variations on the runic alphabet to create secret writings, for divination, protection and spell casting. Traditionally the runes were carved onto wood, stone or bone and considered extremely sacred.

For this exercise you will create your own unique set of `rune style` symbols.

First make a list of questions you would like answered and jot them in your notebook, trying to make them as diverse as possible.

109

The idea is for you to end up with a list of your own symbolic rune style patterns to cover many different scenarios.

Take your notebook outside with you. Find a tree with lots of twigs and spreading branches. Here goes.

- ❖ Call in your guides.
- ❖ Breath Balance.
- ❖ Make a spy hole in your fist and stand under the tree.
- ❖ Peer through your spyhole, moving it around until you find a point where the twigs or branches cross. You will probably be better focusing further away from the trunk. *(This is easier in autumn and winter when there are few leaves on the trees but can still be done where leaves aren`t too dense.)*
- ❖ Soft focus.
- ❖ Ask permission of the tree for it to share its insights.
- ❖ Ask your first question. It could be anything for example: Will I move home within the next year?

- ❖ Take note of the first intersection you see through your spyhole. Jot down in your notebook the shape of the twig joint – remembering the question associated with it.
- ❖ The next step is to interpret from your own intuition/psychic senses what this symbol represents.
- ❖ Take note of any feelings, sensations, thoughts, images, words which pop into your mind.
- ❖ Remember your first impression is the correct one.
- ❖ Ask another question and follow the same process.
- ❖ Keep going for as long as you are getting results. If you find the insights drying up, give thanks to the tree and close the session down for now.
- ❖ Try again at another time, keep working at it until you have built up a wide selection of unique runic symbols.
- ❖ Create a section in your symbolism journal for runic tree symbols based on the shapes you discovered and your own system.

If this exercise resonates with you, you could then paint your runic symbols onto little flat stones or gemstones for your own unique set of divination runes. Pop them into a drawstring bag and use them for readings.

Look up traditional runes and their meanings for curiosity sake, see how they compare with yours. If they are similar – then wow! Either your psychic abilities are absolutely on point, or you were Odin in a past life!

Chapter 27
Automatic Psychic Writing

You can use this method for answering personal questions by tapping into your higher self, to contact your spirit guides, or communicating with spirit for a mediumship reading. When interacting with spirit you may receive words from the deceased person psychically for you to transcribe in your own handwriting, or spirit may utilise your arm for them to write through. This would then appear on the page as their handwriting.

Automatic writing or psychography is a way of channelling information. You may wish to use it for creative inspiration, answering life journey questions when you are unsure of the way forward; or if you are keen to develop your psychic mediumship skills, then this is another powerful tool.

Prepare your sacred space using your normal method. Either cleansing with white sage smudge sticks, burning some incense, clearing with a singing bowl, playing relaxing music.

Within your dimly lit room have a candle for the table centre - choose a candle colour which works for psychic connection, white, silver or gold. You will need several large pieces of paper A3 or larger and a pen which flows freely and doesn't need a great deal of pressure to write with. Fibre tipped pens work well.

To prepare for your automatic writing exercise, with your non-dominant hand, start by signing your name over and over to loosen up. This will help access the creative side of your brain and disengage your conscious mind. Write down any random thoughts which may be popping in and out to purge the daily chit chat and exterior concerns. When you feel ready to start spread your large sheet of paper out on the surface in front of you.

If doing this automatic writing as a reading for a friend explain to them what you are doing – if you are self-conscious about this, you can ask your friend to focus on slowing down their breathing at the same time as you do. Maybe give them a crystal to hold in their hand, suggest they infuse it with their energy.

You can then hold their crystal in your other hand whilst you carry out your automatic writing helping to make a connection.

- ❖ Put your protection in place.
- ❖ **Breath Balance**.
- ❖ Soften your vision.
- ❖ Know that your higher-self will protect you from any unwanted energies along with your guides.
- ❖ Visualise connecting with the purest source of vibrant universal light, way up above you – feel its power invigorating you.
- ❖ As you breathe in, sense it pouring in through the top of your head energising your entire being.
- ❖ Soft focus your eyes on the candle.
- ❖ Then gently transfer your soft focused attention to the page.
- ❖ Transfer the pen to your dominant hand.
- ❖ Direct the energy down into your writing arm.
- ❖ Let your arm rest loosely over the page – let go of any tension.

❖ Be clear whether you wish to communicate with your higher-self or the spirit world.

❖ Focus on your questions.

❖ You can ask these one by one either aloud or internally.

❖ Start by using simple questions which prompt a yes or no answer.

❖ If you are connecting to someone in spirit continue to sense their energy pouring into your higher-self at the crown of your head, where your guides will filter it for you.

❖ Allow the pure golden light from your guides and angels to flood down into your heart centre.

❖ Once a connection is made you can become more specific in your requests.

❖ What is your name? Age? How are you related to ....? When did you pass?

❖ Feel the energy pouring down into your arm. Then, when you feel your arm and hand starting to tingle, allow the words to flow to your paper.

❖ Often you will find patterns and drawings emerging before any words start to come through.

❖ Try and keep your neck straight as this will help the transfer of information to run straight down to your writing arm.

❖ Detach from the process – release any expectation.

❖ Don't analyse at this stage - keep writing.

❖ If you are doing this for a friend, ask them to give you the questions they would like answered beforehand so that you are not disturbed during the process.

❖ With practice you will be able to stay in a trance state and communicate while continuing with your automatic writing.

❖ Do not worry if you only receive pictures and no words.

❖ Sometimes the writing will be illegible, but you will have a clear knowing of what the meaning is. Occasionally you can receive a communication from someone who was not literate in life. If you suspect this is the case, then ask them if they are able to write and for them to indicate with an X if they cannot. In this case you can ask them the question: *"If you could write what would you like to say? Tell me the words as if you could write."*

This is to release the fixation on their behalf, and they will then transfer their words via your higher-self. You will end up with **their** words – **your** handwriting.

❖ Once the communication seems to have naturally trailed off, thank your guides and spirit.

❖ If you choose to finish the session earlier, be courteous, you could say, *Thank you. Goodbye, I now disconnect from this session,* or whatever feels appropriate to you.

❖ Bring yourself out of your meditative state. Clapping your hands together or stamping your feet on the ground will bring you back to full awareness.

❖ Shake your hands as if you are flicking water from them to disconnect completely.

Automatic writing can be quite draining. Don't push it too far for the first few times.

Build up slowly until you can sustain a longer connection.

If at any time during the process you are uncomfortable with the energy coming through, then call upon Archangel Michael and your guides to close the communication safely on your behalf. This is unlikely to happen if you have put your protection in place at the beginning but good to know for peace of mind.

Brilliant! – If speaking to spirit is not your bag then pick up your quill and prepare to channel the next best seller!

Chapter 28
Psychic Detective Work

Take an object which belongs to you and ask a friend to hide it in another room. A piece of jewellery, or keys are good examples. Whilst they are hiding it put your protection in place.

- ❖ **Breath Balance.**
- ❖ Soft focus your vision.
- ❖ Activate your third eye centre.
- ❖ Imagine a `mini you` jumping onto their shoulder and acting as a camera. Watch them with your third eye, see where they place the object. You will have your eyes closed whilst you carry this out but allow all your senses to engage.
- ❖ Allow the sensations to come to you smell, hear and see everything they are doing as they place the object.
- ❖ When they return it is your turn to actually go into the room.
- ❖ See if you can retrace their footsteps, exactly as you remotely viewed it.

❖ If this method doesn't take you to your object, then take a few deep breaths to centre yourself and start moving around the room slowly.

❖ Ask yourself a sequence of questions. Am I warm? Am I cold? Is it high up?

❖ Stop. Close your eyes and feel the response. Is the item low down? Is it inside something? Is it on top of something? Is it underneath something?

❖ Check in with your gut for the answers. If you get a definite yes, for example, is it underneath something? Then allow yourself to feel and know the texture of the item it is beneath. Is it soft or hard? Does it have a weave – like a fabric? If so, would that fabric make you feel hot or cold?

❖ Go through a process of elimination obtaining as much detail as you can, then ask your higher self to paint a clear picture of where the object is stored.

❖ Similar to the process of remote viewing, you can either draw a picture on a blackboard in your mind`s eye, draw a physical picture, or if you believe you have been given a clear image – trust your gut and say where the item is hidden.

Don't be disheartened if you are not able to get the correct image first time. The most important thing is to trust the messages you receive. Ultimately you could expand this skill. If someone else has lost something or a person/animal has gone missing, do the same process to find the location – you can do this!

If this exercise has inspired you, there are many remote viewing websites which offer coded targets for you to focus on. Once you receive the impressions you then click on the target code and it will reveal a picture of the secret location.

Another skill under your belt – another step towards tuned in brilliance!

Chapter 29
Psychic Pigeon Post

This exercise pulls together the learning of all the previous exercises. Now it is time to trust your intuitive and psychic skills.

- ❖ Ask a friend to contact you telepathically within a given period – for example: between the hours of 8am and 8pm on an agreed day. Ask them to send you a simple clear message about something you would not guess.
- ❖ Ask the Sender - to imagine in detail a little movie of the story they are trying to impart. They can say the words aloud, describing the image and colour within it, so, it becomes really vivid.
- ❖ Then ask the sender, in their minds eye to place the piece of film in an envelope and give it to a homing pigeon then see themselves sending the pigeon up into the sky and flying towards your location.
- ❖ Receiver - At your end, sit quietly and slow your breathing. **Breath Balance.**

- ❖ Imagine you are looking up into the sky and you see, feel, hear the pigeon flying towards you. Know that it comes into land and you take the envelope from its beak and open it.
- ❖ Take out the film and place it into a projector. With eyes closed. What do you see, hear, feel? What is the message? What is the mood of the message?
- ❖ Record any feelings, sounds, smells.
- ❖ Report back to your friend – see if any of the elements are correct.

Keep practising! You are teetering on the edge of magnificence.

Chapter 30
What Happens Now?

You have moved a long way towards psychic awakening. With practice you will find that you are perceiving psychic information without having to try so hard.

You will probably notice the more in tune you become with the unseen world around you, the less you are likely to gravitate towards junk food, alcohol and high caffeine drinks. This sounds really boring - but you will begin to be more aware of your reactions to low vibration foods before you eat them. You will know instinctively if something you are about to eat is going to lower your vibration.

It is highly documented that in pregnancy we sometimes get peculiar cravings. The reality is that we are often spot on with detecting vitamin or mineral deficiencies in our diet at that time.

We seem to know exactly what we and the growing foetus require. During pregnancy, we spend more time tuning in to the little person we are growing inside us.

We take notice of fluctuations and changes in our body, movement and sensations. As the baby`s natural instinctive abilities are building in preparation for their arrival we are perhaps brought back into vibrational alignment with the pure state that we also came into the world with.

Once you have honed your psychic skills. You may find you have a more acute awareness of what is good for you and what definitely is not. Trust that you are correct. Of course, it goes without saying that your intuition should not override the need to seek the appropriate professional help if you are unwell or feel you may have a serious medical condition. You can always mention your `gut feeling` if, your health practitioner is open to it. I have been pleasantly surprised at how many doctors and consultants ask the question *"What do **you** think it may be?"*

It seems there is a new generation of medical professionals who are more open to a holistic way of diagnosis. Combining alternative or complimentary medicine with tried and tested traditional methods now seems more common place.

Now you have worked your way through the little exercises in this book you may feel inspired to take your psychic development further. Should you decide that you would really like to go on to become a psychic reader or medium then you have a good grounding. It is worth joining a local spiritual development group – it gives you the opportunity to polish your skills, learn about professional ethics, most importantly it gives you a support network of likeminded individuals. Visit your local spiritualist church if you are thinking of mediumship as your path. Have readings from others so that you can get a feel for the way to carry out - or not to carry out readings. Maybe start reading for friends of friends to ease yourself in. Utilise the methods, you have learned. Start with your protection mantra, **Breath Balance** and softened vision.

You could always ask for them to remove a piece of jewellery or give you their keys to hold throughout the reading for a better connection.

Start by tuning into their aura to help you relax into the reading. Be chirpy and friendly and put them at their ease. If they look tense it is always worth introducing some light humour.

If you can make them laugh it helps to dissolve any resistance and gives you access to their energy field (they have already given permission by asking for a reading) which helps you to access them psychically. It also builds an energetic bridge between the two of you to enable relevant information to flow.

Inevitably you will sometimes have clients who are there because a friend suggested it, and consequently may not be fully present or open to the reading. Although subliminally they have already accepted that a reading will be beneficial otherwise; they wouldn`t have come to you, they could be out to sub-consciously sabotage the reading. If you have a persistent `No that doesn't fit` - `No that name means nothing` client, then there can be many reasons for this:

- ❖ They are fearful of what they may hear from you or spirit. What you may uncover.
- ❖ They are fearful of the possibility that you will be right, and they may have to accept that you are genuine.
- ❖ They are fearful that it goes against their belief system or their conditioning.

❖ They are fearful that your reading will bring emotions to the surface that they have been trying to keep under control.

❖ They are fearful that they will find it is time to let go of their grief.

❖ They genuinely feel no connection with anything you have said.

You have a responsibility to be gentle and compassionate, but it does not mean you must accept rudeness or negativity. Always respect your own boundaries – If you wouldn't accept something outside of your `readings space` then it is even more important not to accept it within it. You have created a sacred place for them to feel safe – you should feel the same.

If your client seems closed from the outset of your reading, then use your skills to gently break down the barriers as mentioned above.

If, your client started with an openness but seems to be shutting down during a reading this could be because you have hit on a truth – take notice of their body language.

It is normal to cover or protect the area of the body which feels threatened in some way. i.e. arms folded over chest – protecting the heart, a hand covering the solar plexus may indicate their fight or flight fear centre has been activated, and they are feeling anxiety. If they keep glancing away or frequently closing their eyes, they are trying to shut you out.

If any of these warning signs are cropping up, respect their boundaries – ask if they would like to close the session. Thank them for allowing you to work with them. Close down by grounding yourself. Ask your guides to ensure you have separated yourself energetically from the other person's energy field. Wash your hands as a symbolic cleansing process.

Go have a well-earned cuppa! If you don't use loose tea, you could always burst open a tea bag and read the tea leaves! You Tasseographer you!

If you decide using these skills professionally is not for you – then you should be feeling some level of empowerment and better awareness of the energies moving round you. When you go about your daily routine try to use some of the skills you have practiced.

The more you practice the stronger your sense of self will become. Your creativity levels should improve. Being in touch with the energetic world around us gives us the advantage of receiving higher quality information for balanced decision making and feeling a little more in control of our destiny. If you can find the time practice your breathing meditation regularly. It helps to quieten your mind and is a great de-stresser.

Why not invite some friends around and start your own psychic evenings to try out the exercises in this book? Although, I would not advise drinking alcohol whilst carrying out psychic work – you could always round the evening off with a few Proseccos and a bowl of pork scratchings.

Remember! We are all psychic, sentient, intuitive beings – it is not a gift – it is our natural state. Be the best you can be! It is so worth the effort. Thank you for joining me on this journey to re-boot your natural super-skills. I hope these exercises have proved food for thought and fun.

Be kind - Be liberated – Be a unicorn!

Glossary of Terms

Aeromancy – *Cloud reading – interpreting the shapes in cloud formations for guidance and divination.*

Affirmations - *Carefully formatted statements repeated over and over, believed to instigate positive personal change.*

Aura - *An invisible field of energy or emanation, an atmosphere or feeling that radiates from someone or something.*

Ceromancy – *Candle wax divination – interpreting melted wax formations to foretell the future.*

Clairaudience – *Clear hearing.*

Claircognizance – *Clear knowing.*

Clairessence - *Clear smelling.*

Clairgustance – *Clear tasting.*

Clairolfaction – *Clear smelling.*

Clairsentience – *Clear feeling.*

Clairvoyance – *Clear sight or seeing.*

Crystallomancy – *Fortune telling by gazing into a crystal ball and interpreting the shapes and images within.*

Divination – *To foretell or predict by reading signs, events, or omens.*

Electro-magnetic radiation – *Energy waves radiating through space such as microwaves, infra-red and radio waves etc.*

Geopathic stress - *A disturbance in earth's natural energies and magnetic field.*

Guided Visualisation – *Guided by another person or oneself to create images and sensations in the mind.*

Higher-self – *A person`s spiritual self.*

Intuition- *Instinctive understanding or knowing.*

Premonition – *A strong feeling that something is going to happen. Previous notice or forewarning.*

Psychic - *Faculties or phenomena inexplicable by natural laws, such as the ability to predict the future or know what other people are thinking.*

Psychic Medium – *Someone who receives and passes on messages from the spirit world.*

Psychography - *Automatic writing is the ability of an individual to produce written words from a spiritual, supernatural or subconscious source without consciously writing them.*

Psychometry - *The ability to discover facts about an event or person by touching inanimate objects associated with them.*

Pyromancy – *Fire gazing – interpreting the shapes in flames and fire embers for guidance and divination.*

Scrying - *A form of divination where you peer at or into a reflective surface or suitable medium to receive images for prophecy or guidance.*

Sensory Perception – *The awareness of things through our five senses, hearing, vision, taste, smell and touch.*

Sixth sense – *An extra sense beyond those considered the normal five senses.*

Spiritual Enlightenment - *A final spiritual state in which everything is understood and there is no more desire or suffering.*

Supernatural – *An event attributed to some force beyond scientific understanding.*

Symbolism - *Marks, signs, words or patterns that represent an idea, object, or relationship.*

Tasseography – *Fortune telling by reading the shapes and symbols in tea leaf residues at the bottom of a tea cup.*

"The world is full of magic things patiently waiting for our senses to grow sharper"
William Butler Yeats 1865 – 1939 Irish poet.

@AuthorRadley

We hope you enjoyed this book – If you wish to stay informed on upcoming books, events, workshops etc: please visit the website and sign up for our newsletter. Thank you for reading.

www.author-radley.co.uk

Printed in Poland
by Amazon Fulfillment
Poland Sp. z o.o., Wrocław

48997414R00081